Making Candy

Turkish Delight, Turkish Marzipan and Almond Dragée Recipes

By
Brenda Van Niekerk

Copyright © 2012 Brenda Van Niekerk
All rights reserved.
Second Edition 2017

Seond Edition 2018

ISBN-13:978-1508820512
ISBN-10:1508820511

Content

DRAGEES RECIPES 2

Dragées 3

Chocolate Almond Dragées 4

Badem Ezmesi (Turkish Marzipan) 7

TURKISH DELIGHT RECIPES 8

Apple Walnut Turkish Delight 10

Apricot Walnut Turkish Delight 12

Black Currant Turkish Delight 15

Cherry Turkish Delight 17

Cherry Walnut Turkish Delight 20

Coconut Macadamia Turkish Delight 23

Ginger Orange Turkish Delight 25

Hazelnut Turkish Delight 28

Lavender Turkish Delight 31

Lemon Almond Turkish Delight 33

Lemon Turkish Delight 36

Mint Turkish Delight 39

Orange Turkish Delight 41

Peach Pistachio Turkish Delight 44

Pistachio Turkish Delight 47

Rhubarb Turkish Delight 49

Rose Turkish Delight 52

Strawberry Turkish Delight 55

Sujuk (Nut Jelly) 57

Dragées Recipes

Dragées

Ingredients

375 ml water

750 ml sugar

750 ml almonds

Method

Combine the water and sugar together in a saucepan.

Stir the mixture to dissolve the sugar.

Add the almonds.

Stir constantly.

Simmer the mixture to allow the excess syrup to evaporate.

Make sure the almonds are evenly coated with syrup.

Remove from the heat.

Spread the syrup coated almonds evenly onto a greased baking tray.

Roast the almonds at 120 degrees F for 30 minutes.

Remove the almonds from the oven.

Leave the almonds to cool.

Store the Almond Dragées at room temperature.

Chocolate Almond Dragées

Ingredients

375 ml water

750 ml sugar

750 ml almonds

Chocolate (melted)

Cocoa powder (for dusting Dragées)

Method

Combine the water and sugar together in a saucepan.

Stir the mixture to dissolve the sugar.

Add the almonds.

Stir constantly.

Simmer the mixture to allow the excess syrup to evaporate.

Make sure the almonds are evenly coated with syrup.

Remove from the heat.

Spread the syrup coated almonds evenly onto a greased baking tray.

Roast the almonds at 120 degrees F for 30 minutes.

Remove from the oven.

Leave the almonds to cool completely

Combine the cooled nuts and ½ the melted chocolate together.

Stir the nuts vigorously in the melted chocolate so that the nuts clump together.

Break the nuts apart into individual nuts.

Refrigerate the nuts for a few minutes to set the chocolate.

Remove the chocolates from the refrigerator.

Combine the nuts with the remaining melted chocolate.

Stir the nuts vigorously in the melted chocolate so that the nuts clump together.

Break the nuts apart into individual nuts.

Refrigerate the nuts for a few minutes to set the chocolate.

Dust the chocolate almond Dragées with cocoa powder.

Store the chocolate almond Dragées at room temperature.

Badem Ezmesi (Turkish Marzipan)

Ingredients

750 ml ground almonds

874 ml sugar

750 ml water

10 ml lemon juice

Method

Combine the sugar and water over together in a saucepan.

Boil until the syrup has thickened.

Stir occasionally.

When the syrup begins to darken add the lemon juice.

Test the syrup in a little water - the syrup should not spread in the water.

Remove from the heat. Leave to cool.

Beat the syrup mixture with an electric beater.

Once the mixture has stiffened and is white add the ground almonds.

Place the dough onto a marble countertop.

Roll the dough into small rolls about a centimeter long.

Turkish Delight Recipes

Apple Walnut Turkish Delight

Ingredients

1 box granulated gelatin

500 ml sugar

83 ml apple juice

37,5 ml lemon juice

250 ml boiling water

187 ml walnuts (chopped)

Few drop apple green food coloring

5 ml apple extract

Icing sugar to dust Turkish Delight

Method

Soak the gelatin in the 83 ml apple juice five minutes.

Place the boiling water, sugar, gelatin mixture, apple green food coloring, apple extract and lemon juice into a saucepan.

Stir until the gelatin has dissolved.

Boil 20 for minutes and remove from heat.

When nearly cold, add the walnuts.

Pour the mixture into a loaf pan which has been rinsed with cold water.

Leave at room temperature until slightly jellied.

Refrigerate overnight.

Loosen the sides with a wet spatula.

Remove the jellied mixture from the pan.

Dust with icing sugar.

Cut into squares.

Roll the squares in icing sugar.

Store the Turkish Delight in airtight container at room temperature.

Apricot Walnut Turkish Delight

Ingredients

    1 box granulated gelatin

    125 ml apricot juice

    225 ml boiling apricot juice

    25 ml lemon juice

    500 ml sugar

    125 ml walnuts (chopped)

    125 ml candied apricots (chopped)

    Icing sugar to dust Turkish Delight

Method

Soak the gelatin in the 125 ml apricot juice five minutes.

Place the boiling apricot juice, lemon juice, sugar and gelatin mixture into a saucepan.

Stir until the gelatin has dissolved.

Boil the mixture for 20 minutes.

Remove from the heat.

When nearly cold, add the walnuts and the candied apricots.

Pour the mixture into a loaf pan which has been rinsed with cold water.

Leave at room temperature until slightly jellied.

Refrigerate overnight.

Loosen the sides with a wet spatula.

Remove the jellied mixture from the pan.

Dust with icing sugar.

Cut into squares.

Roll the squares in icing sugar.

Store the Turkish Delight in airtight container at room temperature.

Black Currant Turkish Delight

Ingredients

    1 box granulated gelatin

    125 ml blackcurrant juice

    250 ml boiling water

    500 ml sugar

    125 ml blackcurrants

    Icing sugar to dust Turkish Delight

Method

Soak the gelatin in the blackcurrant juice five minutes.

Place the boiling water, sugar and gelatin mixture into a saucepan.

Stir until the gelatin has dissolved.

Boil the mixture for 20 minutes.

Remove from the heat.

When nearly cold, add the blackcurrants.

Pour the mixture into a loaf pan which has been rinsed with cold water.

Leave at room temperature until slightly jellied.

Refrigerate overnight.

Loosen the sides with a wet spatula.

Remove the jellied mixture from the pan.

Dust with icing sugar.

Cut into squares.

Roll the squares in icing sugar.

Store the Turkish Delight in airtight container at room temperature.

Cherry Turkish Delight

Ingredients

120 ml cherry juice

1 box granulated gelatin

500 ml sugar

250 ml boiling water

5 ml cherry extract

187 ml green and red glace cherries (chopped)

Pink food coloring

Method

Soak the gelatin in the cherry juice five minutes.

Place the boiling water, sugar, gelatin mixture, cherry extract and pink food coloring into a saucepan.

Stir until the gelatin has dissolved.

Boil 20 for minutes and remove from heat.

When nearly cold, add the glace cherries.

Pour the mixture into a loaf pan which has been rinsed with cold water.

Leave at room temperature until slightly jellied.

Refrigerate overnight.

Loosen the sides with a wet spatula.

Remove the jellied mixture from the pan.

Dust with icing sugar.

Cut into squares.

Roll the squares in icing sugar.

Store the Turkish Delight in airtight container at room temperature.

Cherry Walnut Turkish Delight

Ingredients

    120 ml cherry juice

    1 box granulated gelatin

    500 ml sugar

    250 ml boiling water

    5 ml cherry extract

    187 ml walnuts (chopped)

    Pink food coloring

Method

Soak the gelatin in the cherry juice five minutes.

Place the boiling water, sugar, gelatin mixture, cherry extract and pink food coloring into a saucepan.

Stir until the gelatin has dissolved.

Boil 20 for minutes and remove from heat.

When nearly cold, add the walnuts.

Pour the mixture into a loaf pan which has been rinsed with cold water.

Leave at room temperature until slightly jellied.

Refrigerate overnight.

Loosen the sides with a wet spatula.

Remove the jellied mixture from the pan.

Dust with icing sugar.

Cut into squares.

Roll the squares in icing sugar.

Store the Turkish Delight in airtight container at room temperature.

Coconut Macadamia Turkish Delight

Ingredients

    6 ml lemon juice

    500 ml sugar

    530 ml water

    2,5 ml cream of tartar

    125 ml cornstarch

    9 ml rosewater

    Few drops pink food coloring

    250 ml macadamia nuts (chopped)

    Icing sugar to dust Turkish Delight

    Desiccated coconut to dust Turkish Delight

Method

Combine the lemon juice, sugar and 187 ml water together in a saucepan.

Stir constantly until the sugar dissolves.

Bring to boiling point.

Reduce the heat.

Simmer the mixture until the mixture reaches 240 degrees F.

Remove from the heat.

Combine the cream of tartar, cornstarch and the remaining water together in a saucepan.

Stir until the mixture is smooth.

Bring to boiling point.

Stir the mixture constantly until the mixture has thickened.

Add the lemon mixture.

Stir constantly while cooking for 5 minutes. Reduce the heat.

Simmer for 50 minutes. Stir frequently.

When the mixture has become a golden color add the rosewater.

Stir in a few drops of food coloring and the macadamia nuts.

Pour the mixture into a loaf pan which has been rinsed with cold water.

Leave at room temperature until slightly jellied.

Refrigerate overnight.

Loosen the sides with a wet spatula.

Remove the jellied mixture from the pan.

Dust with icing sugar. Cut into squares.

Roll the squares in the desiccated coconut.

Store the Turkish Delight in airtight container at room temperature.

Ginger Orange Turkish Delight

Ingredients

    6 ml lemon juice
    500 ml sugar
    530 ml water
    2,5 ml cream of tartar
    125 ml cornstarch
    9 ml orange water
    Few drops orange food coloring
    125 ml crystallized ginger (chopped)
    Icing sugar to dust Turkish Delight

Method

Combine the lemon juice, sugar and 187 ml water together in a saucepan.

Stir constantly until the sugar dissolves.

Bring to boiling point.

Reduce the heat.

Simmer the mixture until the mixture reaches 240 degrees F.

Remove from the heat.

Combine the cream of tartar, cornstarch and the remaining water together in a saucepan.

Stir until the mixture is smooth. Bring to boiling point.

Stir the mixture constantly until the mixture has thickened.

Add the lemon mixture.

Stir constantly while cooking for 5 minutes.

Reduce the heat. Simmer for 50 minutes. Stir frequently.

When the mixture has become a golden color add the orange water.

Stir in a few drops of food coloring and the crystallized ginger.

Pour the mixture into a loaf pan which has been rinsed with cold water.

Leave at room temperature until slightly jellied.

Refrigerate overnight.

Loosen the sides with a wet spatula.

Remove the jellied mixture from the pan.

Dust with icing sugar.

Cut into squares.

Roll the squares in icing sugar.

Store the Turkish Delight in airtight container at room temperature.

Hazelnut Turkish Delight

Ingredients

    1 box granulated gelatin

    500 ml sugar

    83 ml orange juice

    37,5 ml lemon juice

    250 ml boiling water

    Zest of 1 orange

    187 ml hazelnuts (chopped)

    Pink food coloring

Method

Soak the gelatin in the orange juice five minutes.

Place the boiling water, sugar, gelatin mixture, pink food coloring and lemon juice into a saucepan.

Stir until the gelatin has dissolved.

Boil 20 for minutes and remove from heat.

Add the zest.

When nearly cold, add the hazelnuts.

Pour the mixture into a loaf pan which has been rinsed with cold water.

Leave at room temperature until slightly jellied.

Refrigerate overnight.

Loosen the sides with a wet spatula.

Remove the jellied mixture from the pan.

Dust with icing sugar.

Cut into squares.

Roll the squares in icing sugar.

Store the Turkish Delight in airtight container at room temperature.

Lavender Turkish Delight

Ingredients

    6 ml lemon juice

    500 ml sugar

    530 ml water

    2,5 ml cream of tartar

    125 ml cornstarch

    9 ml lavender extract

    Few drops purple food coloring

    Icing sugar to dust Turkish Delight

Method

Combine the lemon juice, sugar and 187 ml water together in a saucepan.

Stir constantly until the sugar dissolves.

Bring to boiling point.

Reduce the heat.

Simmer the mixture until the mixture reaches 240 degrees F.

Remove from the heat.

Combine the cream of tartar, cornstarch and the remaining water together in a saucepan.

Stir until the mixture is smooth. Bring to boiling point.

Stir the mixture constantly until the mixture has thickened.

Add the lemon mixture.

Stir constantly while cooking for 5 minutes.

Reduce the heat.

Simmer for 50 minutes.

Stir frequently.

When the mixture has become a golden color add the lavender extract.

Stir in a few drops of food coloring.

Pour the mixture into a loaf pan which has been rinsed with cold water.

Leave at room temperature until slightly jellied.

Refrigerate overnight.

Loosen the sides with a wet spatula.

Remove the jellied mixture from the pan.

Dust with icing sugar.

Cut into squares.

Roll the squares in icing sugar.

Store the Turkish Delight in airtight container at room temperature.

Lemon Almond Turkish Delight

Ingredients

    17 oz unflavored gelatin
    1500 ml cold water
    250 ml sugar
    5 ml salt
    1500 ml hot water
    Zest from 1 lemon
    Juice from 1 lemon
    250 ml almonds (chopped)
    Few drops yellow food coloring
    Icing sugar to dust Turkish Delight

Method

Soften the gelatin in the cold water.

Combine the sugar, salt and hot water together in a saucepan.

Bring to boiling point.

Stir constantly.

Add the gelatin mixture.

Lower the heat.

Simmer for 20 minutes – do not stir.

Remove from the heat.

Add the lemon zest, lemon juice, almonds and yellow food coloring.

Leave for 3 minutes.

Pour the mixture into a loaf pan which has been rinsed with cold water.

Leave at room temperature until slightly jellied.

Refrigerate overnight.

Loosen the sides with a wet spatula.

Remove the jellied mixture from the pan.

Dust with icing sugar.

Cut into squares.

Roll the squares in icing sugar.

Store the Turkish Delight in airtight container at room temperature.

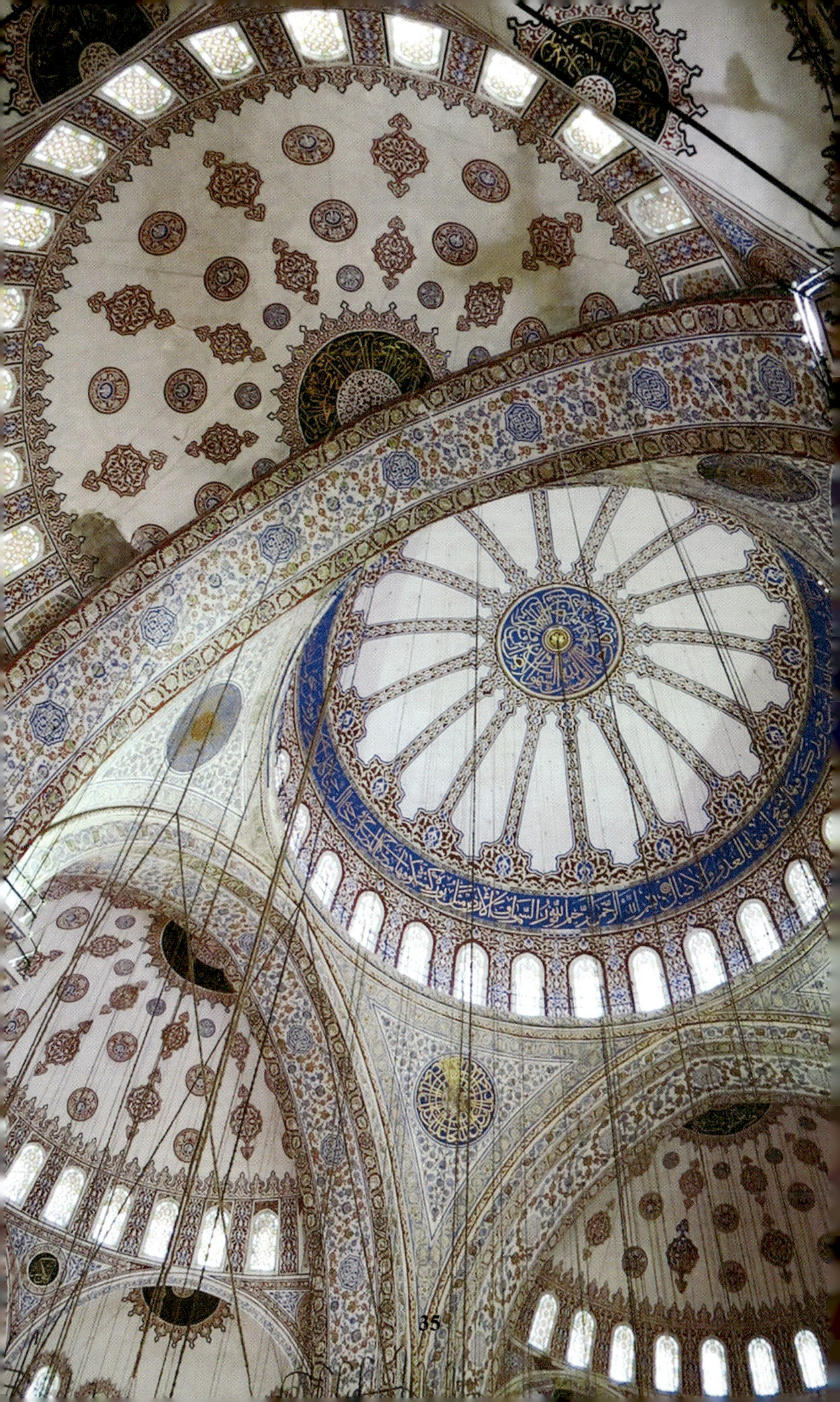

Lemon Turkish Delight

Ingredients

    17 oz unflavored gelatin

    1500 ml cold water

    250 ml sugar

    5 ml salt

    1500 ml hot water

    Zest from 1 lemon

    Juice from 1 lemon

    Few drops yellow food coloring

    Icing sugar to dust Turkish Delight

Method

Soften the gelatin in the cold water.

Combine the sugar, salt and hot water together in a saucepan.

Bring to boiling point.

Stir constantly.

Add the gelatin mixture.

Lower the heat.

Simmer for 20 minutes – do not stir.

Remove from the heat.

Add the lemon zest, lemon juice and yellow food coloring.

Leave for 3 minutes.

Pour the mixture into a loaf pan which has been rinsed with cold water.

Leave at room temperature until slightly jellied.

Refrigerate overnight.

Loosen the sides with a wet spatula.

Remove the jellied mixture from the pan.

Dust with icing sugar.

Cut into squares.

Roll the squares in icing sugar.

Store the Turkish Delight in airtight container at room temperature.

38

Mint Turkish Delight

Ingredients

    1 box granulated gelatin

    125 ml cold water

    250 ml boiling water

    500 ml sugar

    250 ml fresh mint leaves (chopped)

    Few drops green food coloring

    Icing sugar to dust Turkish Delight

Method

Soak the gelatin in the cold water for five minutes.

Place the boiling water, sugar and gelatin mixture into a saucepan.

Stir until the gelatin has dissolved.

Boil the mixture for 20 minutes.

Remove from the heat.

When nearly cold, add the mint leaves.

Pour the mixture into a loaf pan which has been rinsed with cold water.

Leave at room temperature until slightly jellied.

Refrigerate overnight.

Loosen the sides with a wet spatula.

Remove the jellied mixture from the pan.

Dust with icing sugar.

Cut into squares.

Roll the squares in icing sugar.

Store the Turkish Delight in airtight container at room temperature.

Orange Turkish Delight

Ingredients

- 6 ml lemon juice
- 500 ml sugar
- 530 ml water
- 2,5 ml cream of tartar
- 125 ml cornstarch
- 9 ml orange blossom water
- Few drops orange food coloring
- Icing sugar to dust Turkish Delight

Method

Combine the lemon juice, sugar and 187 ml water together in a saucepan.

Stir constantly until the sugar dissolves.

Bring to boiling point.

Reduce the heat.

Simmer the mixture until the mixture reaches 240 degrees F.

Remove from the heat.

Combine the cream of tartar, cornstarch and the remaining water together in a saucepan.

Stir until the mixture is smooth.

Bring to boiling point.

Stir the mixture constantly until the mixture has thickened.

Add the lemon mixture.

Stir constantly while cooking for 5 minutes.

Reduce the heat. Simmer for 50 minutes.

Stir frequently.

When the mixture has become a golden color add the orange blossom water.

Stir in a few drops of food coloring.

Pour the mixture into a loaf pan which has been rinsed with cold water.

Leave at room temperature until slightly jellied.

Refrigerate overnight.

Loosen the sides with a wet spatula.

Remove the jellied mixture from the pan.

Dust with icing sugar.

Cut into squares.

Roll the squares in icing sugar.

Store the Turkish Delight in airtight container at room temperature.

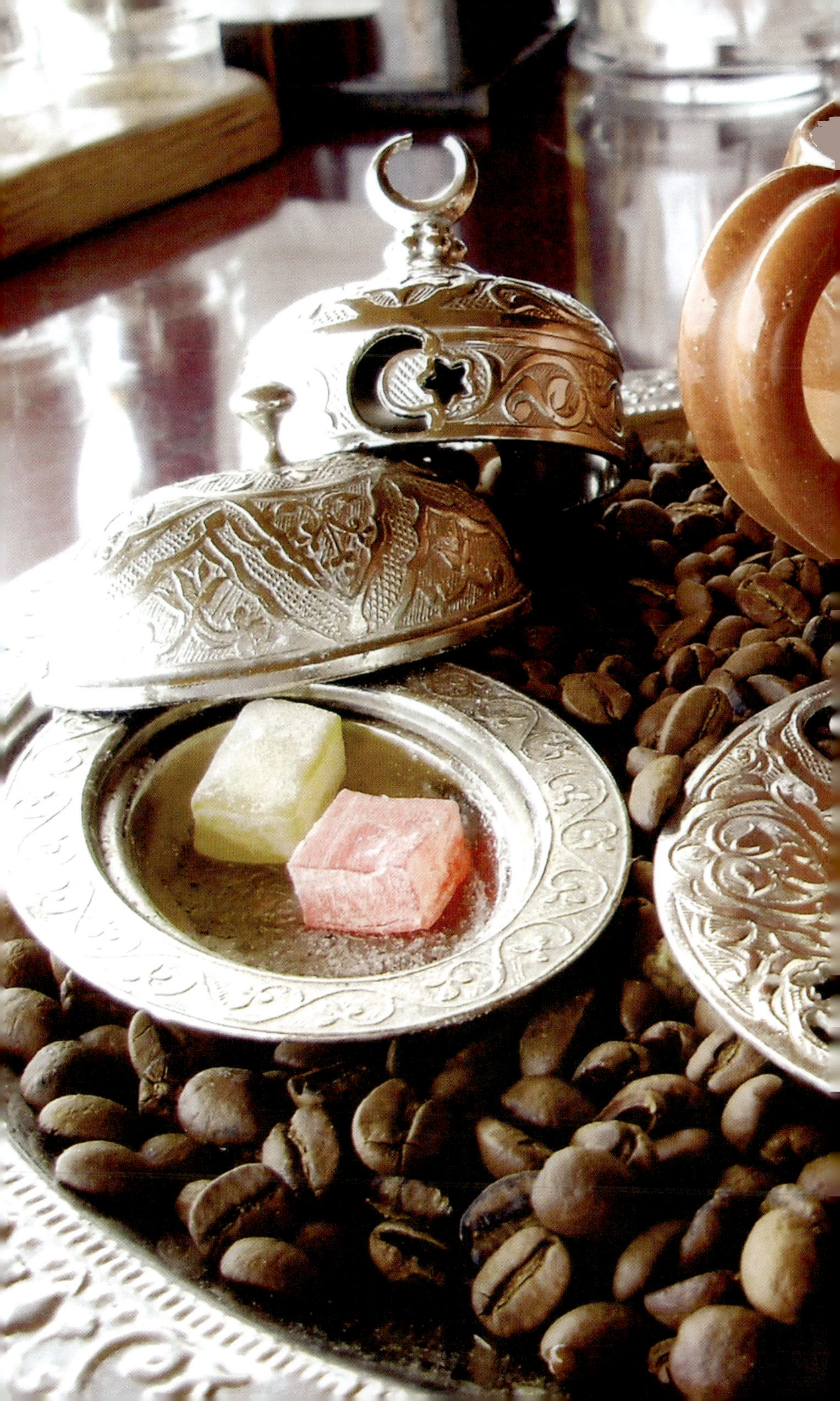

Peach Pistachio Turkish Delight

Ingredients

1 box granulated gelatin

500 ml sugar

120 ml peach juice

225 ml boiling peach juice

25 ml lemon juice

Zest of 1 orange

187 ml pistachio nuts (chopped)

Few drops orange food coloring

Method

Soak the gelatin in the peach juice five minutes.

Place the boiling peach juice, sugar, gelatin mixture, orange food coloring and lemon juice into a saucepan.

Stir until the gelatin has dissolved.

Boil 20 for minutes and remove from heat.

Add the zest.

When nearly cold, add the pistachio nuts.

Pour the mixture into a loaf pan which has been rinsed with cold water.

Leave at room temperature until slightly jellied.

Refrigerate overnight.

Loosen the sides with a wet spatula.

Remove the jellied mixture from the pan.

Dust with icing sugar.

Cut into squares.

Roll the squares in icing sugar.

Store the Turkish Delight in airtight container at room temperature.

46

Pistachio Turkish Delight

Ingredients

17 oz unflavored gelatin

1500 ml cold water

250 ml sugar

5 ml salt

1500 ml hot water

Juice from 1 orange

250 ml pistachio nuts (chopped)

Few drops green food coloring

Icing sugar to dust Turkish Delight

Method

Soften the gelatin in the cold water.

Combine the sugar, salt and hot water together in a saucepan.

Bring to boiling point.

Stir constantly.

Add the gelatin mixture.

Lower the heat.

Simmer for 20 minutes – do not stir.

Remove from the heat.

Add the pistachios, orange juice and green food coloring.

Leave for 3 minutes.

Pour the mixture into a loaf pan which has been rinsed with cold water.

Leave at room temperature until slightly jellied.

Refrigerate overnight.

Loosen the sides with a wet spatula.

Remove the jellied mixture from the pan.

Dust with icing sugar.

Cut into squares.

Roll the squares in icing sugar.

Store the Turkish Delight in airtight container at room temperature.

Rhubarb Turkish Delight

Ingredients

- 1 box granulated gelatin
- 500 ml sugar
- 83 ml orange juice
- 37,5 ml lemon juice
- 250 ml boiling water
- Zest of 1 orange
- 187 ml almonds (chopped)
- Pink food coloring
- 500 ml rhubarb (peeled and chopped)
- Icing sugar to dust Turkish Delight

Method

Soak the gelatin in the orange juice five minutes.

Place the boiling water, sugar, gelatin mixture, rhubarb, pink food coloring and lemon juice into a saucepan.

Stir until the gelatin has dissolved.

Boil 20 for minutes and remove from heat.

Pour the syrup mixture through a strainer to remove the rhubarb pieces.

Add the zest.

When nearly cold, add the almonds.

Pour the mixture into a loaf pan which has been rinsed with cold water.

Leave at room temperature until slightly jellied.

Refrigerate overnight.

Loosen the sides with a wet spatula.

Remove the jellied mixture from the pan.

Dust with icing sugar.

Cut into squares.

Roll the squares in icing sugar.

Store the Turkish Delight in airtight container at room temperature.

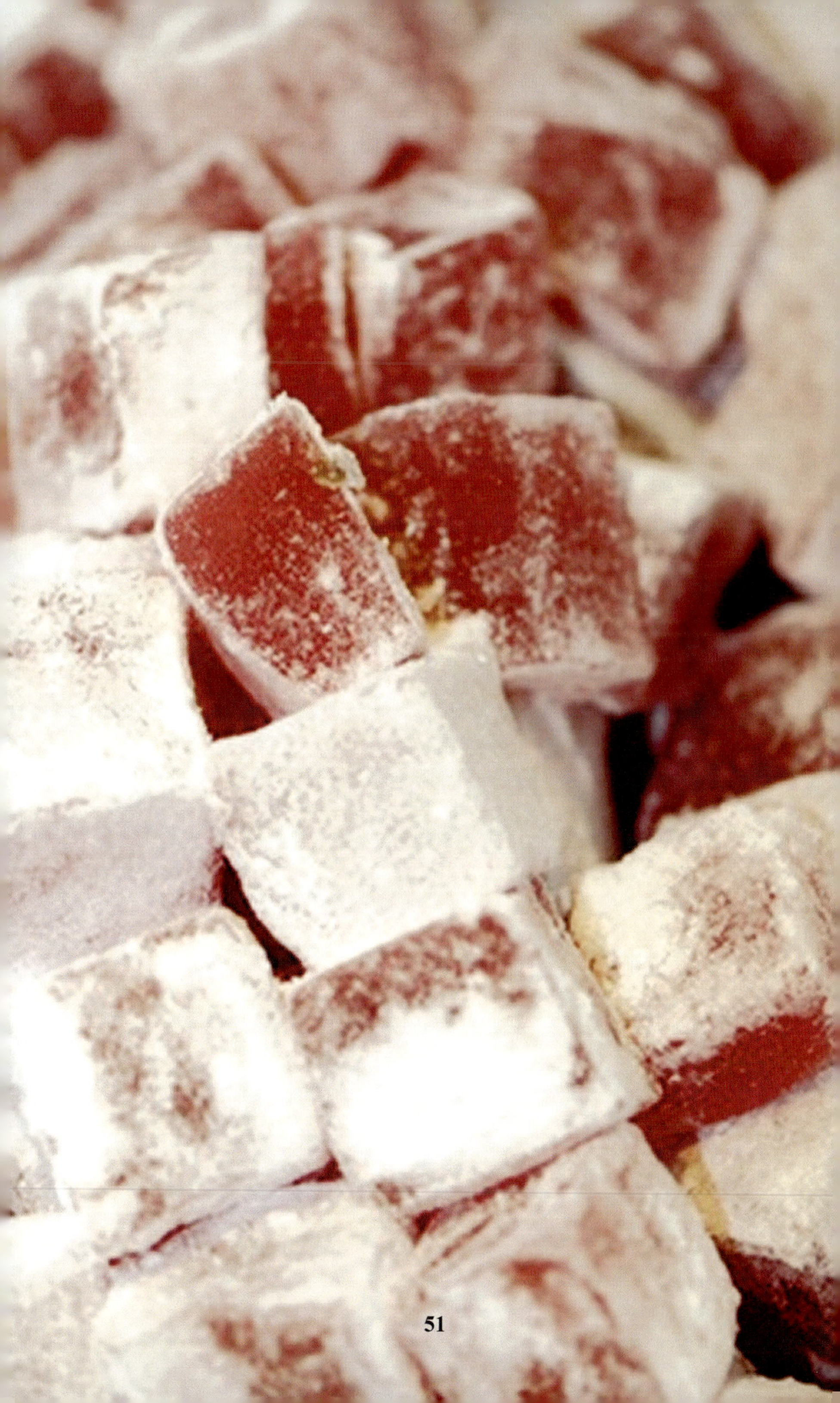

Rose Turkish Delight

Ingredients

    6 ml lemon juice

    500 ml sugar

    530 ml water

    2,5 ml cream of tartar

    125 ml cornstarch

    9 ml rosewater

    Few drops pink food coloring

    Icing sugar to dust Turkish Delight

Method

Combine the lemon juice, sugar and 187 ml water together in a saucepan.

Stir constantly until the sugar dissolves.

Bring to boiling point. Reduce the heat.

Simmer the mixture until the mixture reaches 240 degrees F.

Remove from the heat.

Combine the cream of tartar, cornstarch and the remaining water together in a saucepan.

Stir until the mixture is smooth.

Bring to boiling point.

Stir the mixture constantly until the mixture has thickened.

Add the lemon mixture.

Stir constantly while cooking for 5 minutes.

Reduce the heat.

Simmer for 50 minutes.

Stir frequently.

When the mixture has become a golden color add the rosewater.

Stir in a few drops of food coloring.

Pour the mixture into a loaf pan which has been rinsed with cold water.

Leave at room temperature until slightly jellied.

Refrigerate overnight.

Loosen the sides with a wet spatula.

Remove the jellied mixture from the pan.

Dust with icing sugar.

Cut into squares.

Roll the squares in icing sugar.

Store the Turkish Delight in airtight container at room temperature.

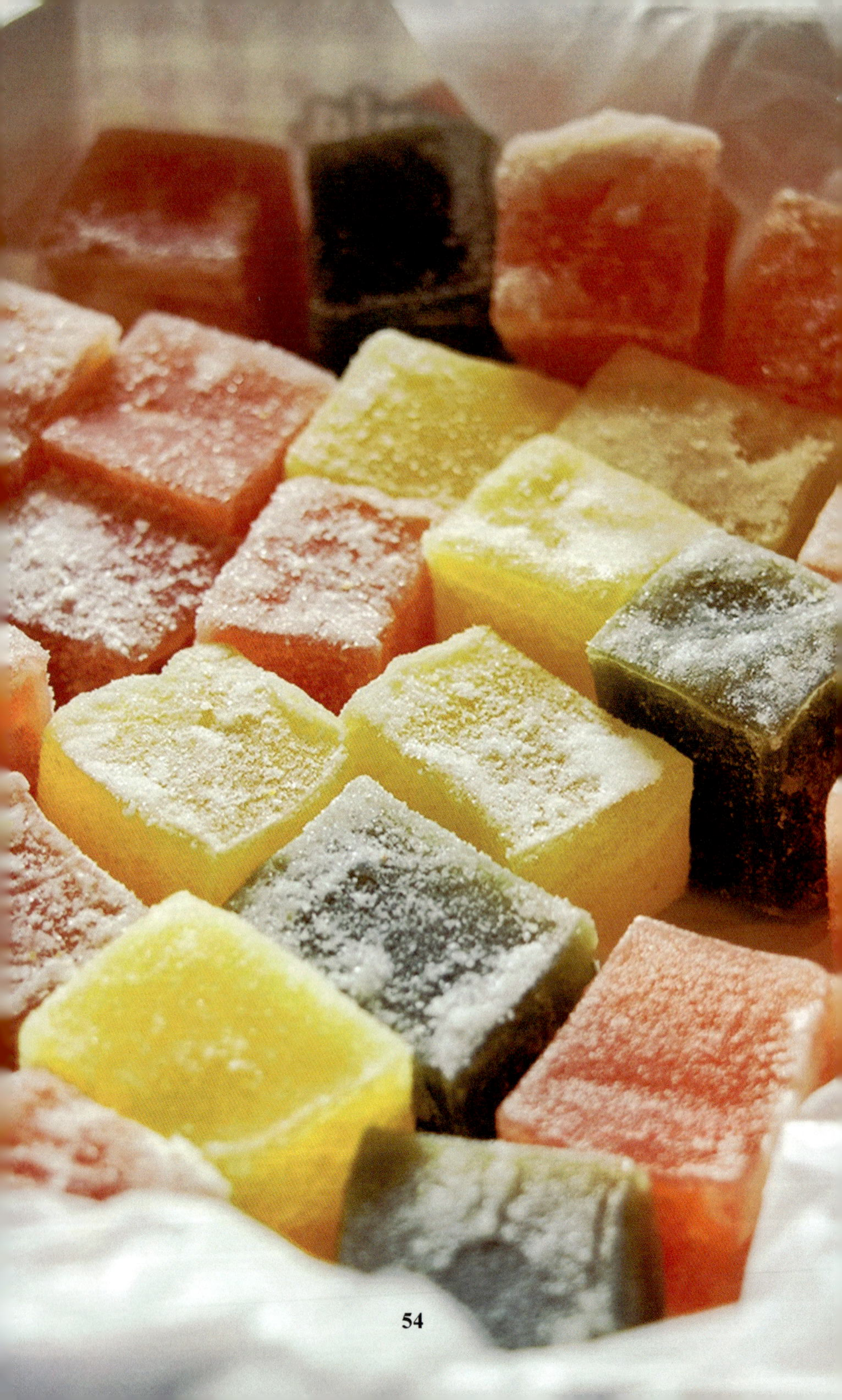

Strawberry Turkish Delight

Ingredients

- 6 ml lemon juice
- 500 ml sugar
- 530 ml water
- 2,5 ml cream of tartar
- 125 ml cornstarch
- 9 ml strawberry extract
- Few drops pink food coloring
- Icing sugar to dust Turkish Delight

Method

Combine the lemon juice, sugar and 187 ml water together in a saucepan.

Stir constantly until the sugar dissolves.

Bring to boiling point.

Reduce the heat.

Simmer the mixture until the mixture reaches 240 degrees F.

Remove from the heat.

Combine the cream of tartar, cornstarch and the remaining water together in a saucepan.

Stir until the mixture is smooth. Bring to boiling point.

Stir the mixture constantly until the mixture has thickened.

Add the lemon mixture.

Stir constantly while cooking for 5 minutes.

Reduce the heat.

Simmer for 50 minutes.

Stir frequently.

When the mixture has become a golden color add the strawberry extract.

Stir in a few drops of food coloring.

Pour the mixture into a loaf pan which has been rinsed with cold water.

Leave at room temperature until slightly jellied.

Refrigerate overnight.

Loosen the sides with a wet spatula.

Remove the jellied mixture from the pan.

Dust with icing sugar.

Cut into squares.

Roll the squares in icing sugar.

Store the Turkish Delight in airtight container at room temperature.

Sujuk (Nut Jelly)

Ingredients

- 10 ml saffron threads
- 500 ml boiling water
- 75 ml wheat starch
- 220 ml water
- 880 ml water
- 220 g sugar
- 12 walnuts (ground fine)

Method

Combine the saffron threads and the boiling water together.

Cover the mixture and leave to infuse.

Combine the wheat starch and water together.

Mix well.

Combine the wheat starch mixture and the remaining water together in a saucepan.

Bring the mixture to boiling point.

Stir continuously.

Reduce the heat.

Cook for 10 minutes.

Add the sugar.

Stir until the sugar dissolves.

Cook for 10 minutes.

Remove from the heat.

Add the saffron infusion.

Mix well.

Add the ground walnuts.

Mix well.

Pour the mixture into a serving dish.

Refrigerate and serve cold.

59

Printed in Great Britain
by Amazon